WORLD MUSIC:
A Source Book for Teaching

by Lynne Jessup

Illustrations by Mary McConnell

World Music: A Source Book for Teaching
Copyright © 1988 Lynne Jessup

Illustrations © 1988 Mary McConnell
Cover designed by Connie Reid/ReidGraphics
Cover illustration by Mary McConnell

*In order to best serve your needs, this listing will be updated via an
Annual Supplement. If you know of or have used any materials you
feel should be included in the next update, kindly send all specifics
(including availability) to the publisher at the address below.*

ISBN 0-937203-19-X Original Paperback Edition

World Music Press
Multicultural Materials for Educators
PO Box 2565 Danbury CT 06813
(203) 748-1131

Printed in the United States of America
First Printing July 1988

Library of Congress Cataloging-in-Publication Data
Jessup, Lynne, 1944-
    World music : a source book for teaching/ by Lynne Jessup :
illustrations by Mary McConnell. -- Original pbk. ed.
        p.   cm.
    Bibliography: p.
    ISBN 0-937203-19-X (pbk.) :
    1. Folk music--Bibliography. 2. Folk music--Discography. 3. Folk
music--Film catalogs. 4. Folk music--Instruction and study.
    5. Folk music--Instruction and study--Audio-visual aids.   I. Title.
ML128.F74J47 1988   88-12225
016.7817--dc19   CIP   MN

CONTENTS

PREFACE

Teachers don't always have the time or left over energy to prowl the local book stores and record shops for some new piece of music that will be "just the right thing" to incorporate into their teaching in order to bring their students sounds from other places or cultures.

Many teachers want to include world music into their music or social studies classes, but sometimes can't find suitable materials for their unique teaching situation.

While this source book is by no means comprehensive, it is meant as a guideline to assist teachers in the selection process. I have included titles that I have used in my teaching, and in some cases have mentioned specific examples and at what age or level they work best. I have made my selections on the basis of what is useful to the teacher, yet is authentic in its portrayal of the music culture in question.

New materials are being produced much more rapidly than a few years ago, plus video tapes have made films much more accessible. I hope that if you have suggestions for other materials to include that you will write to me in care of the publisher, so that this book can be updated periodically, and in doing so, continue to serve your needs as a teacher.

Lynne Jessup

Bibliography

GENERAL

Anderson, William M. & Joy E. Lawrence
  1985 **Integrating Music Into The Classroom**
      Belmont, CA: Wadsworth. 356 pages.
      Chapter 7, "Integrating Music with the Study of Peoples and
      Places" suggests activites for including world music in the
      classroom.

Belefonte, Harry
  1962 **Songs Belefonte Sings**
      New York: Duell, Sloan and Pierce. 197 pages.
      An excellent collection of folk songs, including songs from many
      countries and cultures.
      (out of print)

Dasher, Richard
  1975 **Music Around the World**
      Portland, Maine: J. Weston Walch. 72 pages.
      A very brief but useful survey with suggested musical activities
      for several cultures of Asia, Africa, Europe and America.

Diagram Group
  1976 **Musical Instruments of the World**
      New York: Facts on File, Inc.. 320 pages.
      A pictorial encyclopedia, catagorized by the Sachs-Hornbostel
      system. A **must** for school libraries for student and teacher
      reference.

George, Luvenia A.
  1987 **Teaching the Music of Six Different Cultures**
      Danbury, CT: World Music Press. 236 pages.
      Includes African, Afro-American, American Indian, Jewish, Hawaiian, Mexican,
      and Puerto Rican music and culture with teaching strategies,
      suggested reading, listening examples and audio visual lists. Tape.

Goodkin, Doug
  1985 **Sally Go 'Round The Sun**
      San Francisco: Doug Goodkin. 24 pages.
      A delightful set of classroom tested lessons designed for the
      Orff instrumentarium. A booklet and tape set available from
      San Francisco School 300 Gavin St., San Francisco CA 94134

1986 **Mango Walk**
San Francisco: Doug Goodkin. 37 pages.
A second collection of music suitable for elementary grades using
the Orff instrumentarium. A booklet and tape set (see above
address)

Haywood, Charles
1966 **Folk Songs of the World**
New York: John Day Co.. 320 pages.
An outstanding collection of songs from all over the world, with
introductory information on the music and a good bibliography.

Hood, Mantle
1971 **The Ethnomusicologist**
New York: McGraw Hill. 386 pages.
A thorough introduction to methods of ethnomusicology research;
a "must read" for any student of ethnomusicology but may be too
in-depth for general teaching needs.

Malm, William P.
1967 **Music Cultures of the Pacific, Near East and Asia**
Englewood Cliffs, N.J.: Prentice-Hall. 169 pages.
An overview of the music of each culture with information relating
to the study of music as a world-wide phenomenon. The best survey
published. (See also Nettl).

Marcuse, Sibyl
1964 **Musical Instruments: A Comprehensive Dictionary**
Garden City, N.Y.: Doubleday. 608 pages.
The most authorative and complete dictionary of musical instruments. For high school or above use.

May, Elizabeth
1980 **Musics of Many Cultures**
Berkeley, CA: University of California Press. 433 pages.
An overview introducing ethnomusicology with recorded examples;
chapters on several areas are written by various ethnomusicologists.
Recorded examples are included with the book.

Miller, Carl S., ed.
1972 **Sing, Children, Sing - Songs, Dances and Singing Games of Many Lands**
New York: Chappell & Co. for UNICEF. 72 pages.
Representative songs from many cultures notated, with lyrics in
in the indigenous language, plus translations. Background information
and descriptions of games are given.

Nettl, Bruno
1965 **Folk and Traditional Music of the Western Continents**
Englewood Cliffs, N.J.: Prentice-Hall. 213 pages.
A survey of the music of ethnic groups in Europe, Africa and the
peoples of North, Central and South America; with the Malm book,
a complete survey of the world is provided.

Reck, David
1977 **Music of the Whole Earth**
NY: Charles Scribner's Sons, 545 pages. (out-of-print; avail. in libraries)
Wide-ranging look at sound, music in context, and instruments of a vast array of
cultures. Organized conceptually rather than by culture. Photos.

Sadie, Stanley, ed.
1980 **The New Grove Dictionary of Music and Musicians**
Washington D.C.: Grove's Dictionaries of Music Inc..
Listed by country; gives an overview of the music, instruments,
ensembles, vocal traditions and other related information. Each
entry is by an ethnomusicologist whose specialty is that country.

Titon, Jeff, general editor
1984 **Worlds of Music**
New York: Schirmer. 325 pages.
Chapters on Native America, Ghana, Black America, Eastern Europe,
and India are written by experts on each area. More selective
and detailed than Malm and Nettl.

AFRICA - Sub-Saharan

Acogny, Germaine
1984 **Danse Africaine - Afrikanisher Tanz - African Dance**
Frankfurt: Verlag Dieter Fricke. 112 pages.
Step by step photographs of dance positions, exercises, and steps
that will break down stereotypes of African dance.

Adzinyah, Abraham, Dumisani Maraire, Judith Cook Tucker
1986 **Let Your Voice Be Heard! Songs from Ghana and Zimbabwe**
Danbury CT: World Music Press. 144 total pages.
A variety of songs from two different culture areas of Africa
that are teachable and authentic. The accompanying tape is excellent.

Ajibola, J.O.
1974 **Orin Yoruba - Yoruba Songs**
Ile-Ife, Nigeria: University of Ife Press. 126 pages.
A compilation of sacred and secular songs, with western notation.
Lyrics are in Yoruba with pronunciation guide and translations.

Amoaku, W.K.
1971 **African Songs and Rhythms for Children**
London: Schott. 32 pages.
Songs from Ghana with lyrics, translations and transcriptions for
percussion using Orff-Schulwerk methods. Authentic, yet approachable.
Folkways recording FC 7844 is a companion to the book.

Bebey, Francis
1975 **African Music: A People's Art**
New York: Lawrence Hill. 184 pages.
A discussion of the role of musicians and griots, plus a survey
of African music and instruments.

Berliner, Paul
    1981   **The Soul of Mbira: Music and Traditions of the Shona People of Zimba**
            Berkeley: University of California.
            The construction, history, music and cultural setting of the
            mbira (sansa) are covered. See also the recording by the same
            title.

Blacking, John
    1967   **Venda Childrens Songs**
            Johannesburg: Witwaterstrand University Press. 210 pages.
            A detailed analysis of the songs; many examples are very teachable.
            Several of the texts are translated. Includes a bibliography.

Chernoff, John Miller
    1979   **African Rhythm and African Sensibility**
            Chicago: The University of Chicago Press. 261 pages.
            Emphasis is on rhythm and drumming in the cultural context.
            Overgeneralizes from Ghana to all of Africa at times. A personalized
            view.

Dietz, Betty, and Michael B. Olatunji
    1965   **Musical Instruments of Africa**
            New York: John Day. 115 pages.
            Simply written, suitable for students, it categorizes instruments
            using the Sachs Hornbostel system. With photos and a brief record
            included inside the back cover.

Jessup, Lynne
    1973   **Afro Ensemble: A Beginning Book**
            Fort Worth: Harris. 26 pages.
            A teaching approach to African-style rhythms, with notation and
            background information. Good for beginning or general music classes.

    1983   **The Mandinka Balafon - an Introduction With Notation for Teaching**
            La Mesa: Xylo Publications. 192 pages.
            An introduction to Mandinka xylophone including notation, stories
            illustrations, and teaching techniques. Two accompanying tapes
            provide basic patterns, plus performance style.

Locke, David
    1987   **Drum Gahu**
            Crown Point IN: White Cliffs Media. 142 pages.
            An in-depth study with notation, of "Gahu", a drum ensemble piece
            from the Ewe people of Ghana. Written for instruction purposes,
            companion tapes supplement the written work.

Makeba, Miriam
    1971   **The World of African Song**
            Chicago: Quadrangle Books. 119 pages.
            Many of Makeba's recorded songs are included in this songbook.
            Music notation, background information to each song, and a
            list of the albums is provided.

Nketia, J. H. Kwabena
  1963 **Drumming in Akan Communities of Ghana**
        London: Thomas Nelson. 212 pages.
        A study of drums and drumming; the musical and social aspects,
        uses in the culture, types of ensembles, and notated examples
        of Ghanaian drumming.

  1963 **African Music in Ghana**
        Evanston: Northwestern University Press. 148 pages.
        A general introduction to the music of Ghana, including types of
        folk music, ensembles, and stylistic features with notated
        examples.

  1968 **Our Drums and Drummers**
        Accra: Ghana Publishing House. 48 pages.
        Easily read by children, this small book describes different
        types of drums and their function in the music of Ghana.

  1974 **The Music of Africa**
        New York: W.W. Norton. 278 pages.
        The social and cultural setting of music, musical instruments,
        structures of music, and related arts are covered with emphasis
        on the music of Ghana.

Oliver, Paul
  1970 **Savannah Syncopators - African Retentions in the Blues**
        New York: Stein and Day. 112 pages.
        An excellent outline of aspects of African music of the Western
        Sudan (Sahel) that have been retained in Afro-American music.

Orshan, Allen H.
  1974 **Six African Songs**
        Delaware Water Gap: Shawnee Press. 24 pages.
        The choice of songs is good, however, the accompanying drum patterns
        are used indiscriminately for different songs from different
        countries and ethnic groups.

Serewadda, Moses
  1987 **Songs and Stories from Uganda**
        Danbury CT: World Music Press (reprint 1987). 80 pages.
        Thirteen songs and stories in the Baganda language with translations,
        pronunciation guide, and background information. The illustrations
        are outstanding. Tape includes all songs sung by Serwadda and daughter, and narratives.

Standifer, James and Reeder, Barbara
  1972 **Source Book of African and Afro-American Materials For Music Educators**
        Reston, VA: Music Educators National Conference. 147 pages.
        A very thorough and comprehensive list of sources up to 1972;
        includes concise lesson plans using available recordings.

Tracey, Hugh
  1967 **The Lion on the Path**
        London: Routledge and Kegan Paul. 127 pages.
        Folk tales with songs frim South Africa, written in English,
        with the song lyrics in the original language plus translations
        and notation. Very useful for integrating story and song.

[11]

1970 **Chopi Musicians - Their Music, Poetry, and Instruments**
London: Oxford University Press. 180 pages.
Lyrics, translations, meaning of the music, ensemble arrangement,
instruments, and tuning are included. First edition 1948

Wachsmann, Klaus P.
1971 **Essays on Music and History in Africa**
Evanston, IL: Northwestern University Press. 268 pages.
Several essays by outstanding ethnomusicologists; for teacher
reference, or college level.

ASIA - China and Japan

Berger, Donald P.
1969 **Folk Songs of Japanese Children**
Rutland, VA: Charles Tuttle. 63 pages.
Fifteen songs notated with lyrics in Japanese characters, romanji
and English. Background information on each song.

Dietz, Betty and Thomas Park
1964 **Folksongs of China, Japan and Korea**
New York: John Day. pages.
Includes a record, English translations, background information,
and notes on the scale systems.
.. (not in print)

Gaik See Chew
1986 **Dragon Boat - 20 Chinese Folk Songs for Voices and Instruments**
L ndon: Chester Music. 38 pages.
Almost all the lyrics are given only in English, which detracts
from the collection, however it is still a useful songbook.

Hattori, Ryutaro
1974 **Japanese Folk Songs**
Tokyo: The Japan Times. 168 pages.
Sixty-three well known folk songs notated with lyrics written in
romanized alphabet and characters; English translation given.

Kishibe, Shigeo
1969 **The Traditional Music of Japan**
Tokyo: Kokusai Bunka Shinkokai. 143 pages.
A brief overview of eight major types of Japanese music with many
photographic plates. A good introduction on a scholarly level.
.
Malm, William P.
1959 **Japanese Music and Musical Instruments**
Rutland, VA: Charles E. Tuttle. 299 pages.
Very detailed and authoritative book, clear and useful as a reference.
The discography and annotated bibliography are dated, but it
remains the standard work on Japanese music.

Liang Mingyue
1985 **Music of the Billion: An Introduction to Chinese Musical Culture.**
New York: C.F. Peters. Recommended by colleagues but unreviewed at presstime.

Migita, C.I.
  1970   **The 1st Folk Song Book of Nippon**
         Tokyo: Kawai Gakufu. 185 pages.
         Thirty-six songs notated with the first verse romanized, plus all verses
         in English, kanji, and katakana characters.

Nakamura, Yasuo
  1971   **Noh: The Classical Theater**
         New York: Weatherhill. 248 pages.
         The history of Noh drama, and how it is performed today, written
         in a straightforward manner, with generous illustrations.

Nakano, Ichiro
  1983   **101 Favorite Songs Taught in Japanese Schools**
         Tokyo: The Japan Times. 274 pages.
         Divided historically, the emphasis is on songs composed in the
         first forty years of the 20th century.

Picken, Laurence
  1957   **The New Oxford History of Music: The Music of Far Eastern Asia 1. China**
         London: Oxford University Press. pages 83-134.
         History, instruments, musical forms and religious music are outlined
         clearly with notation and illustrations.

Tsungawa, Shiuchi
  1959   **Japanese Children's Songs**
         Tokyo: Fuji Publishing Co.
         A collection of songs with both Japanese and English lyrics.
         Translations may be oversimplified.

White, F. and Akiyama, K.
  1960   **Children's Songs from Japan**
         New York: Marks Music Corp.
         A variety of songs, most in both Japanese and English, with background
         information. Game songs have instructions. Suitable for grades
         3 to 5.

Yeh Yung-Ching, ed.
  1972   **Chinese Folk Songs**
         New York: ARTS, Inc.   40 pages.
         Twenty authentic Chinese songs, notated with lyrics in characters,
         romanization, and English. Available as a package with a tape and
         booklet of games from World Music Press. Very singable.

*Lai, T.C. and Robert Mok
  1985   **The Jade Flute**
         New York: Schocken Books. 196 pages.
         Readable introduction, giving basic information on instruments and the structure of
         Chinese music. Photos.

**Fukuda, Hanako
  1965   **Favorite Songs of Japanese Children**
         Hollywood: Highland Music Co. (avail. World Music Press) 25 pages.
         Fifteen authentic Japanese children's songs, dance songs and game songs, with dance
         formations, game directions and suggestions for instrumental accompaniment. English and
         romanized Japanese. Brief introductory background notes. Recorded on Bowmar 157.

Bellber, William and Marta Montanez
1981 **Canciones De Mi Isla**
New York: ARTS Inc. 44 pages.
Fourteen traditional songs plus five composed songs from Puerto
Rico, with an accompanying tape that is excellent. Available from
World Music Press with two other booklets covering games and Christr

Brown, Thomas A.
1984 **Afro-Latin Rhythm Dictionary**
Sherman Oaks, CA: Alfred. 48 pages.
A handy reference with notated rhythms for all major latin dances
with photographs of latin percussion instruments plus a glossary.

Courlander, Harold
1960 **The Drum and the Hoe**
Berkeley: University of California Press. 371 pages.
Chapter 18 describes musical instruments of Haiti, drawings of drum
construction, and instruments. Numerous transcriptions of rhythms
and melodies are included.

Davis, Steven and Peter Simon
1977 **Reggae Bloodlines**
London: Heinemann Educational Books. 216 pages.
Vivid photography and intimate description make this book an out-
standing documentary of Reggae music and the Rastifarian belief.
An excellent choice for high school general music reading.

De Cesare, Ruth
Latin American Game Songs
New York: Mills Music.
A music book of game songs in English and Spanish, with game
directions and piano accompaniment. Recorded on Bowmar M-104.

Follow Through Project, UC Santa Cruz
Las Posadas Heritage Unit
Santa Cruz: University of California.
A curriculum outline for midwinter fiestas including The Virgin
of Guadeloupe, Hannukah, Santa Lucia, Santa Claus, and others.

Jekyll, Walter, ed.
1966 **Jamaican Song and Story**
New York: Dover.
Reprinted from a 1907 edition, it includes both the folklore and
folk songs of Jamaica.

Lewin, Olive
1974 **Brown Gal in de Ring 12 Jamaican Folk Songs**
London: Oxford University Press. 16 pages.
Melodies with chords notated plus suggested percussion. Brief
background information given for each song.

Ortiz, Fernando
1955 **Los Instrumentos de la Musica Afrocubana**
Habana, Cuba: Cardenas y Cia. 5 vols.
Extensive descriptions of Afrocuban instruments with drawings of
them. Written in Spanish, suitable for in-depth research.

Paz, Elena
Favorite Spanish Folksongs - Traditional Songs From Spain and Latin America
New York: Oak. 96 pages.
An anthology of Hispanic songs of many styles, with music, lyrics
translations and guitar chords. Background information and sources
given.

Seeger, Pete
1961 **Steel Drums - How to Play Them and Make Them**
New York: Oak. 40 pages.
Practical directions for constructing steel drums are followed by
four transcriptions of varying difficulty. Tuning charts are
included, but making steel drums is not as easy as it sounds!

Sulsbruck, Birger
1987 **Latin American Percussion: Rhythms and Rhythm Instruments**
Chicago: Action Reaction U.S.A..
A book and three tapes provide instruction on latin rhythms which
is both accurate in approach, and understandable by the beginner.
Available from MMB Music.

Travesi, Elena Paz, and Carlos Garcia
Las Posadas
New York: Mills Music.
A music book which includes the play, plus songs with piano
accompaniment.

Yurchenco, H.
1967 **A Fiesta of Folk Songs from Spain and Latin America**
New York: Putnam and Sons.
A good collection of songs in Spanish with translations and background material. Suitable for 5th and 6th grades.

INDIA

Anderson, William M.
1975 **Teaching Asian Musics in Elementary and Secondary Schools**
Danbury, CT: World Music Press. 107 pages.
The basics of raga, tala and musical design in Indian music are
presented with concrete, teachable examples and notation. Tape.

[15]

Krishnaswamy, S.
1967   **Musical Insruments of India**
Boston: Crescendo.   102 pages.
Historical background of the development of Indian musical
instruments preceeds descriptions and photos of the major
instruments.

Massey, Reginald and Jamila
1976   **The Music of India**
New York: Crescendo-Taplinger.   189 pages.
Indian music is described in its cultural context, with concise
information on raga, tala, instruments, and famous musicians.

Shankar, Ravi
1968   **My Music, My Life**
New York: Simon and Shuster.   160 pages.
A personal account of North Indian music, providing the cultural
background as well as basisc information n the music and a manual
for the sitar.

INDONESIA

Anderson, William M.
1975   **Teaching Asian Musics in Elementary and Secondary Schools**
Danbury, CT: World Music Press.   107 pages.
Along with the music of India, this book includes transcriptions
and teaching strategies for Indonesian music which can be adapted
to the Orff instrumentarium. Tape.

Kunst, Jaap
1949   **Music in Java**
The Hague: Martinus Nijhoff. 2 vols. 640 pages.
The classic study of Javanese music, exhaustive and thorough.

Lindsay, Jennifer
1979   **Javanese Gamelan**
Kuala Lumpur: Oxford University Press.   60 pages.
A clear, concise introduction to the instruments and music of the
Javanese gamelan.

ISRAEL AND THE JEWISH DIASPORA

Idelsohn, Abraham Z.
1951   **The Jewish Song Book**
Cincinnati: Cincinnati Publications for Judaism.
Organized by the Jewish religious year, a song collection with
piano accompaniments.

[16]

Idelsohn, Abraham Z.
1967 **Jewish Music in its Historical Development**
New York: Schocken.
Historically traces Jewish music from earliest times to the 20th
century. Divided into songs of the synagogue and folk songs.
Reprint from 1929.

Rothmueller, Aron Marko
1960 **The Music of the Jews - An Historical Appreciation**
New York: A. S. Barnes and Co.
Traditional Jewish music from the 1st to 20th centuries, new Jewish music of the 19th - 20th centuries. One chapter on folk music

Rubin, Ruth
1965 **Jewish Folk Songs**
New York: Oak.
A collection of folk songs in English, (Yiddish words are in the
appendix), with guitar chords. Brief historical information.

Schwadron, Abraham A.
1980 "On Jewish Music" in May, Elizabeth ed. **Music of Many Cultures**
Berkeley CA: University of California Press. pages 284-306
A "capsule view" of Jewish tradition and music, with music
notation, glossary, and sources for further study.

NORTH AMERICA

Ancelet, Barry Jean
1984 **The Makers of Cajun Music**
Austin, TX: University of Texas Press.
A lavishly illustrated book written in both French and English
that covers many currently popular Cajun and Creole musicians.

Bahti, Tom
1967 **Southwestern Indian Ceremonials**
Las Vegas: K. C. Publications.
Describes and illustrates many ceremonies and dances. Emphasis
is not on music, but it gives an excellent cultural overview.

Ballard, Louis
1975 **Music of North American Indians**
Morristown, N.J.: Silver Burdett. 32 pages.
Cultural background, songs, accompaniments and information on
instruments are outlined. Illustrated, includes a map.
Out of print, but among many schools' general music books.

Carawan, Guy and Candie
1966 **Ain't You Got A Right To The Tree Of Life?**
New York: Simon and Schuster. 191 pages.
A wonderful insight with songs descriptive of life on John's
Island, South Carolina in the 60's.

Columbo, John Robert, ed.
1983 **Songs of the Indians II**
Canada: Oberton Press. 100 pages.
Songs from the Northwest coastal region, with an extensive
bibliography and discography for all areas.

Courlander, Harold
1963 **Negro Songs From Alabama**
New York: Oak. 111 pages.
A collection of folk songs and spirituals with transcriptions by
John Benson Brooks.

1963 **Negro Folk Music U.S.A.**
New York: Columbia University Press.
Includes many song transcriptions with the words and melodies,
plus a bibliography and discography.

Curtis, Natalie
1987 **The Indians' Book**
New York: Bonanza Books. 584 pages.
An exhaustive collection of songs notated with words and vocables
including background information.
Reprinted from 1907.

deLerma, Dominique Rene
1970 **Black Music in Our Culture**
Kent, Ohio: Kent State University Press. 263 pages.
Contributions by many authors provide essays on a variety of topics
and curriculum ideas plus sources of information and music,
bibliography, recording and film lists.

Densmore, Frances
1926 **The American Indians and Their Music**
New York: Johnson Reprint Co. - Academic Press.
An early study of dances, games, instruments, songs and song
types, with an analysis of scales used and notated songs.

Driver, Harold E.
1969 **Indians of North America**
Chicago: University of Chicago Press. 632 pages.
An exhaustive study with maps and references. Chapter 12 covers
music and dance.

Feather, Leonard.
1984 **The Encyclopedia of Jazz, New Edition**
New York: De Capo Press.
A reference book on jazz, updated periodically to include new trends and musicians.

Fulton, Eleanor, and Pat Smith
1978 **Let's Slice The Ice: A Collection of Black Children's Ring Games and Cha**
St. Louis, MO.: Magnamusic-Baton. 56 pages.
A good, basic collection of games and songs, with directions for
playing the games. Students often know regional variations.

Garland, Phyl
1969 **The Sound of Soul**
Chicago: Henry Regenery Co. 246 pages.
A good, readable description of soul music with photos and a
discography up to the late '60's.

Gillett, Charlie
1983 **The Sound of The City: The Rise of Rock and Roll**
New York: Pantheon. 515 pages.
A revised and expanded edition, describes the history of rock and
roll from 1954 to 1971 with an accompanying discography.
Reprinted from 1971.

Glass, Paul
1968 **Songs and Stories of the North American Indians**
New York: Grosset and Dunlap. 61 pages.
Good introductory material and songs for the elementary level.
Unfortunately uses English words rather than Indian vocables.

1971 **Songs and Stories of Afro-Americans**
New York: Grosset and Dunlap. 61 pages.
Introductory material plus gospel, blues, and freedom songs.
Suitable for sixth through eighth grades.

Gridley, Mark C.
1985 **Jazz Styles - History and Analysis**
Englewood Cliffs, NJ: Prentice-Hall. 445 pages.
An in-depth study of jazz including styles, history, musicians,
elements of jazz, and a suggested record list.

Handy, W.C. ed.
1972 **Blues: An Anthology**
New York: Collier-McMillan. 224 pages.
A revision of the 1926 original edition, fifty three blues songs
are included with piano accompaniment and guitar chords.

Hentoff, Nat
1961 **The Jazz Life**
New York: Dial Press.
Biographical sketches of famous personalities in jazz.
Very readable, suitable for high school or as a reference.

Herskovits, Melville J.
1968 **The Myth of the Negro Past**
Boston: Beacon Paperbacks.
An outstanding book, that answers misconceptions regarding
Afro-Americans, and concrete examples of African retentions.
Chapter VIII discusses music.

Jackson, Bruce
1972 **Wake Up Dead Man: Afro American Worksongs from Texas Prisons**
Cambridge, Mass.: Harvard University Press. 326 pages.
A thorough treatment of prison worksongs with background
information, function, lyrics, and notation for many of the songs.

Jones, Bessie and Bess Lomax Hawes
1987 **Step It Down**
Athens: Univ. of Georgia Press. 233 pages.
Black American children's songs and games, notated with lyrics, directions for play, and vital background information. A reprinted classic. Pbk and LP avail. World Music Press.

Jones, LeRoi
1963 **Blues People**
New York: Morrow & Co. 244 pages.
An historical approach to the music of Black Americans and its relationship to White America.

1968 **Black Music**
New York: Morrow & Co. 221 pages.
Notes and thoughts on people and events in the jazz world; also includes a discography up to 1968.

Lloyd, A.L., ed.
1965 **Folk Songs of the Americas**
New York: Oak.
Songs notated with lyrics and translations from Canada, U.S.A., Mexico, the Caribbean, Central, and South America.

Lomax, Alan
1960 **The Folk Songs of North America**
Garden City: Doubleday and Co. 620 pages.
Songs from the north, the southern mountains and backwoods, the west and the south with background information and notation.

Lomax, John A. and Alan Lomax
1947 **Folk Song U.S.A.**
New York: Duell, Sloan and Pierce. 512 pages.
Predominantly rural folk songs with notation and suggested musical settings. Topics include: children's songs, war, work, heros, spirituals, and others. "Can'cha Line "Em" (p. 274) is one of the best!

Lovell, John Jr.
1972 **Black Song: The Forge and The Flame**
New York: Macmillan.
A thorough study, divided into three sections on the origin, development, and influence of the spiritual.

Marcus, Griel
1969 **Rock and Roll Will Stand**
Boston: Beacon Press. 182 pages.
A collection of essays on rock and roll giving the flavor of the times, from the early '50s to 1968, with suggested listening.

McGee, Timothy
1985 **The Music of Canada**
Markham, Ont.: Norton-Penguin. 257 pages.
An historical approach to the many types of Canadian music and the ethnic groups that contribute to the culture of Canada.

McIntosh, David
  1974   **Folk Songs and Singing Games of the Illinois Ozarks**
         Carbondale, IL.: Southern Illinois University Press. 119 pages.
         Songs, ballads, and play-party games are notated with directions
         for movement and background information. A recording is included.

Nettl, Bruno
  1954   **North American Indian Musical Styles** - Memoir Series No. 45
         Philadelphia: American Folklore Society. 51 pages.
         Divides North America into six main musical styles and explains
         them. Includes a map and musical examples.

  1962   **An Introduction to Folk Music in the United States**
         Detroit: Wayne State University Press. 126 pages.
         Defines folk music and uses specific examples to illustrate the
         ethnic backgrounds and main types of American folk music.

Oliver, Paul
  1963   **The Meaning of the Blues**
         New York: Collier Books (Macmillan). 383 pages.
         Discusses the meaning and content in blues songs, with an
         extensive discography of the songs quoted.

  1969   **The Story of the Blues**
         Philadelphia: Chilton.
         An historical approach, covering form and history, with emphasis
         on performers. Includes some music examples and several photos.

Sandberg, Larry and Dick Weissman
  1976   **The Folk Music Sourcebook**
         New York: Alfred A. Knopf. 260+xiv pages.
         Divided into sections on "listening", "learning", "playing", and
         "hanging out", includes essays, annotated sources and addresses.
         A "Must have" for folk music fans.

Southern, Eileen
  1983   **The Music of Black Americans: A History**
         New York: Norton. 552 pages.
         A thorough historical coverage from West Africa, through the
         colonial era and up to the present, with an extensive bibliography
         and discography. First printed in 1971.

Stearns, Marshall
  1956   **The Story of Jazz**
         New York: Oxford University Press.
         An excellent historical outline of the growth of jazz, including a
         bibliography, lecture outline, suggested readings and recordings.

Sweet, Jill D.
  1985   **Dances of the Tewa Pueblo Indians**
         Santa Fe, NM: School of American Research Press. 99 pages.
         The focus is on dance rather than music, but the information
         included provides cultural insight and sensitivity for the
         reader. Beautiful color photographs enhance the book.

OCEANIA AND AUSTRALIA

Dean, Beth
1975 **Three Dances of Oceania**
Sydney: Sydney Opera Trust. 96 pages.
Dances of Fiji, Cook Islands, and Banaba, diagrammed step by step
with poetry and translations.

1978 **South Pacific Dance**
Sydney: Pacific Publications. 108 pages.
Extensive photographs illustrate dances from Australia, Melanesia,
Micronesia and Polynesia. Descriptive rather than applicative.

Freedman, Sam
1967 **Maori Songs of New Zealand**
Wellington: Sevenseas Publishing PTY. 164 pages.
An extensive collection of songs, notated and arranged for piano
accompaniment; also includes background information on Maoris and
their legends.

Freeman Moulin, Jane
1979 **The Dance of Tahiti**
Papeete: les editions du pacific. 120 pages.
Beautifully illustrated with chapters on instruments and costumes
plus directions and diagrams for specific dances.

Jones, Trevor
1980 "Traditional Music of the Australian Aboriginies" in May, Elizabeth 1980
Berkeley, CA: University of California Press. pages 154-171
A good introduction, with glossary, bibliography, discography, and
film list.

Kaeppler, Adrienne
1980 "Polynesian Music and Dance" in May, Elizabeth 1980
Berkeley, CA: University of California Press. pages 134-153
Again Elizabeth May's book provides a good introduction to
a specific area, with glossary, bibliography and discography.

1983 **Polynesian Dance - With a Selection for Contemporary Performances**
Honolulu, HI: Alpha Delta Kappa. 110 pages.
Written for classroom teachers, with background information plus
clear instructions and diagrams for specific dances.

Kelly, John M. Jr.
1963 **Folk Songs Hawaii Sings**
Rutland VT: Charles E. Tuttle. 80 pages.
Indiginous songs, plus songs from other Polynesian islands and
Asian immigrants to Hawaii. Lyrics in original languages and English
translations. (out of print)

MacDonald, Dan
1972 **Nihi Ta Fanganta**
Agana, Guam: Insular Arts Council of Guam. 54 pages.
A collection of traditional and composed songs sung by Chamorro
school children of Guam and the Mariana Islands.

McLean, Mervyn
　1971　**Maori Music**
　　　　Wellington: School Publications, Dept. of Education.　32 pages.
　　　　Written for student readers, with specific notes for a listening
　　　　tape.　Covers recited and sung styles of Maori chant.

Roberts, Helen H.
　1967　**Ancient Hawaiian Music**
　　　　New York: Dover.
　　　　Originally written for the Bishop Museum Bulletin 29.
　　　　Reprint from 1926

PHILIPPINES

Pfeiffer, William R.
　1976　**Filipino Music: Indigenous, Folk, Modern**
　　　　Dumaguete City, R.P: Silliman Music Foundation, Inc.　284 pages.
　　　　Songs, epics, and instruments of each island area of the Philippines
　　　　are included, plus information on folk and modern music.　Not in
　　　　print but may be possible to purchase through Cellar Books.

SOUTHEAST ASIA

Morton, David
　1968　**The Traditional Music of Thailand**
　　　　Los Angeles: University of California Press.　47 pages.
　　　　Accompanies recordings by the same title.　Gives commentary and
　　　　analysis.

Pham-Duy
　1975　**Musics of Vietnam**
　　　　Carbondale, IL: Southern Illinois University Press.　161 pages.
　　　　Regional styles, folk songs, music for entertainment, and theater
　　　　music are covered. Songs are translated but not notated.

SOUTH AMERICA - ECUADOR

Brennan, Elizabeth Villarreal
　1988　**A Singing Wind: Five Melodies from Ecuador**
　　　　Danbury, CT: World Music Press　32 pages
　　　　Five traditional Ecuadorian melodies and story in typical arrangements for voice, re-
　　　　corder, guitar, percussion and optional Orff instruments. Lyrics, story and background
　　　　notes in Spanish and English.　Tape includes performance and pronunciation.

Discography

An Anthology of the World's Music
Anthology 4001-5, 6000. By The Society for Ethnomusicology
A series of recordings of particular cultural areas, each recorded
by specialists in the area. See individual listings.

Black Music of Two Worlds
Folkways FE 4062. By John Storm Roberts   1977
A companion to the book by the same title, covering both folk and
popular music of Africa, the West Indies, South America and the USA.

Folk Instruments of the World
Follett L 24. By Moses Asch, ed.
Compiled for educational use, examples are very brief but good,
with notes and line drawings. Out of print but can be found in
school record collections.

Highlights of Folk and Traditional Music of Asia
ACCU UNT01-03.   1983
Songs, instrumental, and dance music provide a cross-section of
Asian music excerpted from a 9 volume record set.
Order from Asian Cultural Center for Unesco.

Instrumental Music of Asia and the Pacific   3 Volumes
ACCU UYH1-1,2,3. By Harumi Koshiba   1979
This three volume set with 121 page booklet, is a exaustive survey
with good recorded examples and accurate background information.
Order from Asian Cultural Center for Unesco.

Songs of Asia and the Pacific   3 Volumes
ACCU series 3-1,2,3. By Fumio Koizumi   1982
Each set contains three cassettes and a ±100 pg. booklet providing
the notation, lyrics and translations for each song.
Order from Asian Culture Center for Unesco.

The Nonesuch Explorer
Nonesuch H7-11. By Teresa Sterne   1971
A survey of the world's music; a sampler from various Nonesuch
recordings. An excellent first purchase.

Africa - Shona Mbira Music   Mhuri yekwaRwizi
Nonesuch H-72077. By Paul Berliner 1977
The first two examples illustrate how mbira music is constructed,
followed by a complete performance with vocal parts also.

Africa East and West
i.e. records ier-6751. By various ethnomusicogists, Mantle Hood, editor 1969
Emphasis on Ghana, plus Nigeria, Rhodesia, Sierra Leone, Zambia and
Uganda; primarily a survey of instrumental music.

African Dances and Games   Seth and Alfred Ladzekpo
S & R 2000.   1969
Ghanaian dances and games accompanied by a manual outlining the
dance movements using diagrams and also Labanotation.

African Dances of the Witwaterstrand Gold Mines
Gallo SGALP 1032&33. By Hugh Tracey
Two volumes include dances and music of miners from several tribes
in South Africa.

African Journey: A Search for the Roots of the Blues   2 Volumes
Vanguard-Sonet SRV 73014,5. By Samuel Charters 1975
Includes examples of the standard, traditional repertoire of the
professional jalis of several Gambian ethnic groups.

African Rhythms and Instruments   3 Volumes
Lyrichord LLST 7328,38,9. By Roberto Leydi 1969
A documentation of the music festival held in Algiers in 1969;
divided generally by volume into West, East, and North Africa.

African Songs and Rhythms for Children   Dennis Allen, Kojo Tetty, W.K Amoaku
Folkways FC 7844. By Dr. W.K. Amaoku 1978
Use in Conjunction with Amoaku, **African Songs and Rhythms**
in the Orff-Schulwerk tradition. The American vocal tone quality
of the woman singer detracts, but doesn't ruin the recording.

African Story Songs   Abraham Dumisani Maraire
University of Washington Press   By U.W. Archives of Music and Dance 1969
The stories are told in English, songs are in Shona. Includes lyrics
with translations; students can learn by singing along.

Afrique Noir
Ocora BAM LD 409A. By Charles Duvelle 1963
An excellent survey of many instruments and playing styles; notes
are in French only, however this is a "must have".

Assalam Aleikoum Africa; Volume Two   Amedee Pierre, the Zoulous, Bony Pascal
Antilles - Island AN 7033. By Catherine Org & Albert Lourdes
A good cross section of the modern folk music and contemporary
popular music being recorded for local use in West Africa.

[25]

Children's Songs From Kenya D. Nzomo and Chorus
Folkways FC 7852.
The songs can be learned by rote from the recording, or the teacher
could transcribe them. Words and translations are provided.

Dance Suites From West Africa CalArts African Ensemble
Zadonu 901. By Kobla Ladzekpo 1985
Group includes Ghanaians and Americans under the direction of Agbi and Kobla Ladzekpo
Provides clear examples for students who want to play in the Ghanaian drum ensemble
style. S.1. b.2 is a good piece to try.

Dumi and the Minanzi Marimba Ensemble Dumisani Maraire
Voyager VRLP 404 S. By Alan Yonge 1977
The full sound of a Shona marimba ensemble, as played by an American
group, including both traditional and contemporary compositions.

Ethiopia: I. Copts
Barenrieter BM 30L 2304. By Jean Jenkins
Music of the Coptic church, including an example of the sistrum.

Ewe Music of Ghana
Asch Mankind Series AHM 4222. By S.K. Ladzekpo 1969
Mainly music to accompany traditional Ewe funerals and dances,
including "Atsiagbekor"; song titles are translated.

Kora Manding - Mandinka Music of the Gambia
Ethnodisc ER 12102. By Roderic Knight 1970
An excellent survey of traditional kora repertoire and songs, with
a booklet of explanatory notes.

Kpanlogo Party Oboade
Tangent TGS 115. By Mike Steyn 1973
Music that makes you want to get up and dance, this recording can
be used to teach basic rhythm patterns or the dance "Kpanlogo".

Mbira Music of Rhodesia Dumisani Maraire
University of Washington UWP 1001. By Robert Garfias 1971
Mbira music of the Shona people of Zimbabwe, with extensive notes
by Maraire explaining "nyunga-nyunga" mbira music.

Miriam Makeba Miriam Makeba
RCA Victor LSP-2267.
"The Click Song" can introduce new language possibilities to
students in need of broader cultural horizons. Songs notated in
Makeba's book, **The World of African Song**

More Drums of Passion - Olatunji
Columbia CS 9307. By Teo Marcero
This recording is useful for an Afro ensemble group to hear the
balance and interrelationship of both vocal and instrumental
parts. Commercialized, but authentic.

Music From the Heart of Africa - Burundi
Nonesuch H-72057. By Guiseppe Coter 1974
An overview of instrumental and vocal music of the Hutu and Masai
peoples recorded before the ethnic fighting of 1972 and 1973.
Compare the drumming style to that of West Africa.

[26]

Musical Instruments 3. Drums

Kaleidophone KMA - 3. By Hugh Tracey 1972

Rhythms, signals and a message, plus tuned drums and drumming for dancing from the Congo and East African areas. Also a good survey to use as a comparison of styles. Originally on Gallo.

Musical Instruments 4. Flutes and Horns

Kaleidophone KMA 4. By Hugh Tracey 1972

A survey of different types of flutes, panpipes, horns, and gourds from Central and South Africa. Originally recorded on Gallo, and re-released by Kaleidophone.

Musical Instruments 5. Xylophones

Kaleidophone KMA 5. By Hugh Tracey 1972

side 1 - pentatonic and hexatonic xylophones; side 2 - heptatonic xylophones. Another Gallo re-released; also in the series are: 1. Strings, 2. Reeds (Mbira), 6. and 7. Guitars.

Musique Dahomennes

Ocora OCR 17. By Charles Duvelle 1963

Excellent examples, with notes in French and photos illustrating a variety of instruments and ensembles. Several of the selections can be used for music listening activities.

Mustapha Tetty Addy Addy, Mustapha Tetty

Lyrichord LLST 7250 and Tangent TGS113. By Mike Steyn

Includes several examples of Ga and Ewe drumming, including master drumming, Ga gongs, "Kolomashi", Gome songs and "Kpanlogo". Addy is considered to be a "chosen one" by his people.

Olatunji! Drums of Passion Olatunji

Columbia CS 8210.

A professional performer in New York, Olatunji retains the elements of Yoruba drumming in a commercial format. A good transitional introduction to African music.

Sing Children Sing - Songs of the Congo

Caedmon TC1644. By Andouche Firmin Ntoumi 1980

Traditional and composed childrens songs recorded in the Congo and produced with the assistance of UNICEF.

Songs of Kenya

African Music Association AMA TR 164. By Hugh Tracey

Praise and dance songs, several of which are suitable for grades 4 through 9.

Sounds of Africa

Verve FTS 3021. By ABC TV News crew and Andrew Tracy 1966

Selections cover a variety of sounds, music and instruments. "Stand Up For Jesus" is an outstanding example of missionary music.

The Many Voices of Miriam Makeba Miriam Makeba

Kapp KS-3274.

This recording can be used in conjunction with Makeba's book which has several of the selections notated. "Zenizenabo" is excellent.

The Music Of Africa
BBC REC 130, and Horizon RDC-4393. By BBC Archives 1971
Music from all areas of Africa, including Arabic, Black African and European influences.

The Music of the Ba-Benzele Pygmies
Barenrieter BM 30 L 2303. By Simkha Arom with G. Taurelle
"Hindewhu" - an example of voice and flute hocketing, was the basis of Herbie Hancock's version of "Watermelon Man" on his **Headhunter** album.

The Soul of Mbira
Nonesuch H-72054. By Paul Berliner 1973
Four mbira traditions of the Shona people of Zimbabwe played by virtuoso soloists and by ensembles. This album is a companion to the book by the same title by Berliner.

Three Chordophone Traditions
Musicaphon BM 2314.
The bagana, krar and masinqo of Ethiopia perform outstanding solos from the traditional repertoire.

Voices Of Africa Saka Acquaye and his African Ensemble
Nonesuch H-72026.
In contrast to the older traditions of Ghana, this is a collection of modern, urban popular, dance, highlife and concert music.

Zombie Fela and the Afrika 70
Mercury SRM-1-3709. 1977
One of the most infamous musicians of Africa, Fela uses his music to make political statements in a hard-driving musical style.

ASIA - China, Japan, and Korea

A Bell Ringing in The Empty Sky Goro Yamaguchi
Nonesuch H-72025. By Peter K. Siegel 1968
Shakuhatchi music of Japan. The tone quality of the instrument and playing style are unique.

Art of the Koto - The Music of Japan Kimio Eto
Electra EKS-7234. By Mark Abramson and Jac Holzman
Includes "Sakura" and other traditional selections, plus three children's songs.

Beating the Dragon Robe - A Traditional Peking Opera
Folkways FW 8883.
Recorded in an authentic style, with English translation and notes provided.

Classical Music of Japan
Electra EKS-7286. By Katsumasa Takasago 1965
A good first choice, covering koto, shakuhatchi, flute, and excerpts from Kabuki, Gagaku, Kagura, Geza and Kyogen, with brief but concise jacket notes.

Flower Dance - Japanese Folk Melodies Noday family, Nakagawa and Oishi
Nonesuch H-72020. By Katsumasa Takasago
Arrangements of traditional folksongs played on the shamisen, koto and percussion.

Japanese Koto Classics Shinichi Yuize
Nonesuch H-72008. By Peter Siegel
A selection of compositions from the koto repertoire with vocal accompaniment.

Japon 3 - Gagaku Oni Gagaku Kai Society
Ocora 558 551. By Akira Tamba 1980
Includes "Etenraku" and "Bairo", two of the pieces most often performed by the ensemble, with notes in English and French. Not a beginning listening lesson, but following the meter can be challenging.

Kodo - Heartbeat Drummers of Japan Kodo
Sheffield Lab. CD-KODO. (compact disk format only)
Contemporary taiko drumming by Kodo, a group of musicians whose music reflects their absolute concentration and dedication. The video by the same title is an excellent presentation.

Music From Korea Volume 1: The Kayakeum Byongki Hwang
East-West Center Press EWS-1001. By Robert Lang 1965
Music composed by the kayakeum performer and accompanied by the changko drum; rhythmic and good for listening, rhythm activities can be developed as listening strategies.

Music From The Kabuki
Nonesuch H-72012. By Katsumasa Takasago
Geza music is the "off-stage" music that accompanies Kabuki, used as incidental music, to set scenes, and at interludes.

O-Suwa - Daiko: Japanese Drums
GREM G 1029.
Drum music from the Suwa valley of Japan that is a part of Shinto rituals and military music; with notes.

Sounds and Music of China
Monitor MFS 525. By Robert Menegoz
Music, sounds of the city, workmen and other aspects of life in China were used to make this soundtrack for the film **Behind The Great Wall.** S. 2, b. 2b is a good work song.

The Azuma Kabuki Musicians Azuma musicians
Columbia ML 4925. By S. Hurok 1954
Nagauta music and arrangements of classic selections of Kabuki music; each piece of music is briefly described on the jacket notes.

An Island Carnival
Nonesuch H-72091. By Krister Malm 1977
Examples chosen clearly illustrate the influences of many ethnic groups from several areas of the world.

Caliente = Hot
New World NW 244. By Rene Lopez 1977
Detailed notes support this recording of Latin music recorded in New York, but truly Puerto Rican and Cuban in its presentation.

Canciones De Mi Isla Doris Duarte
ARTS Inc. 2604. By Tom Maloney
Part of a booklet and tape package, the songs on side one are for children, and are sung in a clear, charming voice by a young singer who students can relate to. Available from World Music Press.

Caribbean Island Music
Nonesuch H-72047. By John Storm Roberts 1972
From rural to urban the record illustrates the Afro-Hispanic, Afro-British, and Afro-French music of several islands. Compliments John Storm Roberts' book **Black Music of Two Worlds.**

Children's Songs and Games from Ecuador, Mexico and Puerto Rico
Folkways FC 7854. By Henrietta Yurchenco
A good album using "real" songs and "real" kids; with lyrics and translations provided in the accompanying notes.

El Conguero - Poncho Sanchez
Concord-Picante CJP-286. By Chris Long 1985
Latin jazz, good for high school general music listening, includes several cuts that could be used in teaching activities.

Marimba Music of Tehuantepec 2 Volumes
U of Washington Press UWP-1001,2. By Robert Garfias 1972
Extensive notes accompany these two volumes of sones played by the marimba ensembles of Oaxaca; includes transcriptions and analysis.

Peter Tosh - Equal Rights
Columbia 34670.
One of the most famous Jamaican reggae singers, Tosh's songs, in the reggae tradition, express political and social unrest.

Rastaman Vibration Bob Marley and the Wailers
Island ILPS 9383.   1976
Marley was instrumental in developing reggae into an internationally recognized style. The messages contained in his songs can be used to illustrate how music is used for social commentary.

Sing Children Sing - Songs of Mexico Ninos Cantores de la Ciudad de Mexico
Caedmon TC 1645. By W. Botsford and R. Zamudio 1980
A usable recording of orchestrated songs for choir, with marimba, Mexican style trumpet, mariachis, and good children's voices.

The Esso Trinidad Steel Band
Warner Brothers WB 1917.   1971
    Steel drumming as a virtuoso art, with a repertoire that includes
    everything from popular songs to Saint-Saens "Aquarium".

The Harder They Come Jimmy Cliff, plus others
Mango (distributed by Capitol) MLPS 9202.
    The soundtrack from the film by the same title; gives a clear
    picture of the cultural background and sound of reggae music.

The Real Bahamas
Nonesuch H-72013. By Peter Siegel and Jody Stecher 1965
    Vocal music intricately interwoven with rhythmic and harmonic
    texture that any choir would envy. A "must listen" for vocal
    groups.

The Real Mexico
Nonesuch H-72009. By Henrietta Yurchenco 1965
    Fiesta music and songs of the Tarascan Indians and mestizos of
    Michaocan province.

This Is Reggae Music
Island ILPS 9251. By Danny Holloway 1974
    An outstanding survey of reggae music including The Wailers, Jimmy
    Cliff, and The Maytals.

Understanding Latin Rhythms   Volume 1 and 2
L P Ventures LPV-337. By Martin Cohen 1974
    Instructional recordings with notation for learning specific
    rhythms on Latin instruments.

INDIA

42 Lessons For Tabla Ustad Keramatullah Khan
Folkways   FM 8369 or CRB 12. By Robert S. Gottlieb 1973
    An instructional recording with a 23 page booklet describing each
    lesson with notation and photographs of hand positions.

Bhavalu - Impressions Palghat Raghu, Subramaniam, and K.V. Narayanswamy
Nonesuch H-72019. By Peter Siegel
    Emphasis on this recording is on South Indian instrumental rather
    than vocal music, with a mridangam solo, and a display of
    virtuosity.

Carnatic Music - The Music of South India K. V. Narayanswamy
World Pacific WPS 21450. By Richard Bock
    The vocal music of South India, sung by a master, with violin,
    mridangam, tabla and tamboura accompaniment. Voice and violin
    volley complex improvisations and immitations back and forth.

Chant The Names of God
Rounder 5008 (38704). By Edward Henry 1981
The often neglected folk traditions of India are well documented in
this recording from north-eastern India; with good notes and
photographs.

Dhyanam - Meditation; South Indian Vocal Music K.V. Narayanswamy
Nonesuch H-72018. By Peter Siegel
Carnatic music at its best with vocal improvisation by the leading
singer of the tradition, accompanied by Subramaniam on the violin.

Drums of North and South India Allaraka, C. Lal, K. Dutta, Ramabhadran, Sivar
World Pacific WPS -21437. By Richard Bock
The virtuosos of Indian drumming, both North and South are presented
on this outstanding recording. Brief notes on the jacket.

Pallavi - South Indian Flute Music Viswanathan, L. Shankar, Ranganathan
Nonesuch H-72052. By Peter Siegel 1973
A plain bamboo flute, the kural is capable of complexity
in the hands of master musician Viswanathan.

Sarangi - the Voice of A Hundred Colors Ram Narayan and Mahapurush Misra
Nonesuch H-72030.
A more subdued sound than other Indian stringed instruments, the
sarangi is a bowed lute of the art music traditions of North India.

Shehnai Recital by Bismillah Khan
Odeon MOAE 113.
The virtuoso of the shehnai, Khan raised the stature of the
instrument from folk to art music.

The Music of India - Sharan Rani
World Pacific WP 1418. By Henry Jacobs 1962
Sarod music, with an excellent tabla solo, illustrating rhythm
cycle changes from fifteen to ten beats.

The Sounds of India Ravi Shankar
Columbia CS 9296.
Shankar begins with a short explanation of Indian music, useful to
the teacher or older student; the selections clearly illustrate
the framework of Indian music.

The Ten Graces Played on the Vina M. Nageswara Rao
Nonesuch H-72027. By Peter Siegel 1968
Three compositions by the famous South Indian composer, Tyagaraja,
clearly illustrate the structure of raga and tala in South Indian
music.

INDONESIA

Dancers of Bali
Columbia ML 4618. By Colin McPhee
An excellent recording with the lavish, shimmering sound of the Balinese gamelan.

Gamelans de Bali
Disques BAM BAM 5.096. By Louis Berthe and B. Yzerdraat 1963
A wide selection of folk gamelans of Bali, with notes in French, plus a bibliography and discography.

Golden Rain
Nonesuch H-72028. By David Lewiston
Side 1 - the massive sound of the Gamelan Gong Kebyar; side 2 - the monkey chant "Ketjak" in a recording sufficiently long to feel the energy and form of the drama.

Javanese Court Gamelan   The court gamelan of Paku Alaman VIII
Nonesuch H-72044. By Robert E. Brown 1971
The gamelan music of central Java (Jogyakarta); notes describe gamelan music in general, plus information on each selection.

Music From the Morning of the World
Nonesuch H-72015. By David Lewiston
A "buy first" record, this survey includes gamelan music, the "Ketjak" monkey chant, folk ensembles, jaws harps and other examples of the music of Bali.

Music of Indonesia
Folkways FE 4406. By Raden Suwanto 1949
A good survey of Indonesian music of Java, Sumatra, Bali and Malaya with brief notes; an old recording however.

Music of the Venerable Dark Cloud
ie ier 7501. By Mantle Hood, Hardja Susilo 1973
Students of the UCLA gamelan ensemble playing in the authentic and traditional style of Central Java; includes a 42 page booklet with notation and background information on gamelans and their music.

The Jasmine Isle
Nonesuch H-72031. By Suryabrata and David Lewiston
A selection of solo gender and full gamean music in the styles of Central Java (Jogjakarta) and Sunda.

ISRAEL AND THE JEWISH DIASPORA

In Israel Today 4 Volumes
> Westminster W-9805,6,10,11. By Deben Bhattachara
>> From India, Morocco, Yemen, Morocco, Tunisia, Spain, and Eastern Europe, Jews have immigrated to Israel, bringing their music with them. Each volume covers a different geographic area.

Jewish Life: The Old Country
> Folkways FG 3801. By Ruth Rubin 1958
>> Extensive notes with texts and translations accompany this collection of Eastern European music recorded by immigrants to New York.

Sing Children Sing - Songs of Israel Children's Orchestra and Choir
> Caedmon TC 1672. By Ammon Roberman 1981
>> A children's choir with full orchestra accompaniment, includes traditional songs plus composed contemporary songs. S. A, b.3. could be worked out for the Orff instrumentarium.

Yeminite and Other Israeli Folk Songs Guela Gill
> Folkways FW 8735.
>> Popular folk songs with lyrics in Hebrew, plus translations into English and background notes.

NORTH AFRICA AND THE MIDDLE EAST

Al Oud - Hamza El Din
> Vanguard VSD 79194.   1965
>> Hamza El Din from The Sudan, is the virtuoso of oud players. The oud is the type of lute from which the guitar developed.

Chants et Dances du Maroc
> Le Chant du Monde LDX 7 4419.
>> Songs and dances of Morocco, including "Ahouache" and "Guedra" from the Atlas Mountain region.

Music and Drum Rhythm from Iran
> Philips 831 216 PY. By Deben Bhattacharya
>> Rhythms used to accompany gymnastics utilizing drums, chains and chanting.

Music of North Africa
> Olympic OL 6107.
>> A good example of urban popular, orchestral music.

Musique Populaire Marocaine
> Disques BAM LD 435. By Jean Mazel
>> Music from the middle Atlas Mountains, Chleu region, and from the Blue People of southern Morocco. Notes in French and English.

[34]

Om Kalsoum - Amal Hyati   (also spelled Umm Kulthum)
   Sono Cairo SC 22105 also recorded on EMI.
      A live performance with audience reaction audible, this is one of
      several of her recordings which illustrate the power of her voice
      and operatic style. Om Kalsoum is a musical legend in Egypt.

The Music of Morocco
   London SW 99485. By Ray Horricks 1968
      Includes the call to prayer, folk music and dances, plus music
      played by entertainers in the square at Marrakesh.

NORTH AMERICA

American Indian Music for the Classroom
   Canyon 3001,2,3,4. By Louis Ballard 1973
      The music of twenty-two tribes is covered on four volumes, plus
      a teaching guide, map, bibliography, and other teaching aids make this a
      very practical package for the teacher. Good for elementary grades.

American Skiffle Bands   The Memphis Jug Band and other jug bands
   Folkways FA 2610. By Samuel B. Charters 1957
      Includes jugs, washboards, kazoos, and washtub bass; a good record
      to illustrate homemade instruments.

Angola Prisoner's Blues   Robert Pete Williams, Hogman Maxey, and Guitar Welch
   Arhoolie 2011. By Dr. Harry Oster 1959
      Recorded at Angola Prison, Louisiana; songs are by actual prisoners
      and have the ring of authenticity.

Anthology of American Folk Music   3 Volumes
   Folkways FA 2951-3. By Harry Smith 1952
      An extensive collection of the folk music of America, with notes.
      Volume 1 - Ballads, Volume 2 - social music, Volume 3 - songs.

Been Here And Gone
   Folkways FA 2659. By Frederic Ramsey, Jr. 1960
      A survey of various early forms and styles, including hollers, work
      songs, blues, and church music. A companion to the book by the same
      title.

Chippewa Grass Dance Songs   Kingbird Singers
   Canyon C-6106.   1973
      Various styles of Chippewa music are recorded with supporting
      information on the music and performers.

Country Gospel Song
   Folkways RBF 19. By Samuel Charters
      Covers religious music and gospel with notes on each section.

Gracias a la Vida Joan Baez
A&M SP 3627.   1974
Lyrics for each song are given in both Spanish and English on the
record liner. An excellent recording; "De Colores" is a classic.

J'etais au Bal
Swallow 6020.   1974
Contemporary Cajun music performed by some of the best known
musicians; recorded in both field and studio settings.

Mongo Santamaria - Soul Bag
Columbia CJ 9653.
A rhythmic blend of Afro-Cuban and Afro-American music, Mongo
Santamaria developed a popular style without loosing the
vitality of his earlier recordings.

Music of the Ozarks
National Geographic 07703. By Marc Aubort 1972
Extensive notes and photographs augment the selections of fiddle,
banjo, guitar, autoharp mountain dulcimer and singing. Lyrics
are included in the notes.

Negro Church Music
Atlantic 1351. By Alan Lomax
Part of the Southern Folk Heritage series, this volume covers
gospel, spirituals, lining out hymns, and a sermon excerpt.
(see also listing under **Southern Folk Heritage Series**).

Negro Folk Rhythms Ella Jenkins
Folkways FC 7654.   1960
Very singable songs by Ella Jenkins and the Goodwill Spiritual
Choir. Lyrics are included in the jacket notes.

Negro Prison Camp Worksongs prisoners at Texas State Prison Farms.
Folkways F- 4475. By Pete Seeger
A classic recording of songs sung by actual prisoners, not polished
but very "real". "Grizzely Bear" is outstanding.

Nootka - Indian Music of the Pacific Northwest Coast
Folkways FE 4524. By Ida Halpern 1974
"Public" songs including paddle songs and warrior songs. Clan
songs include wolf, robin and grizzly bear.

Pueblo Songs of the Southwest
Indian House IH 9502. By Tony Issacs 1972
A variety of dances that were recorded at the Inter-Tribal Indian
Ceremony in Gallup, New Mexico in 1969.

Santana's Greatest Hits Santana
Columbia PC 33050.
Includes his hits that have become classics - "Evil Ways", "Black
Magic Woman" and the more latin "Oye Como Va". Basic rhythms fo
latin percussion can be taught as listening activities.

ongs of Earth, Water, Fire and Sky
New World NW 246. By M. Moore, and C. Heth 1976
One of a five volume survey of major Indian tribal groups, this
volume includes Cherokee, Seneca, Navajo, and Arapaho music.

ongs of Love, Luck, Animals and Magic
New World NW 297. By Charlotte Heth 1977
Another in the series on Native American music, this volume covers
the Yurok and Tolowa peoples of California.

ounds of Indian America
Indian House IH 9501. By Tony Isaacs 1970
A recording of the plains and Southwest Indians made live at the
Gallup Intertribal Ceremonial, with background information and
notes.

ounds of the South
Atlantic 1346. By Alan Lomax
An outstanding recording of vocal and instrumental music of both
Black and White heritage. Connections with Africa are evident.
(see also next listing).

outhern Folk Heritage Series
Atlantic 1346,7,8,9,50,51,52. By Alan Lomax 1959
This excellent series includes: **Sounds of the South, Blue Ridge Mountain
Music, Roots of the Blues, White Spirituals, American Folk Songs
For Children, Negro Church Music** and **The Blues Roll On.**

tep It Down Bessie Jones
Rounder 8004. By Mark Wilson and Bill Nowlin 1979
Recorded by Bessie Jones with children singing the responses. A
booklet included with the record provides the lyrics and page references
to the book by the same title.

he Eskimos of Hudson Bay and Alaska
Folkways FE 4444. By Laura Bolton 1955
Vocal music of the eskimos including songs, stories, children's
games, animal immitations and dance songs.

he Sound of the Delta - A Mississippi Blues Anthology
Testament T-2209. By Norman Daron, Big Joe Williams 1965
Good examples for a lesson on the blues, best for high school level,
performed by some of the most outstanding traditional blues singers.

ime Further Out Dave Brubeck Quartet
Columbia 8490 (reissue). 1961
Classics of jazz using unusual meters including "Unsquare Dance" in
7 8 time.

raditional Blues Sung by Brownie McGhee
Folkways FA 2421. 1960
Good listening examples for lessons on the blues, best for eighth
grade through high school. Lyrics are included in the notes.

OCEANIA AND AUSTRALIA

Fijian Songs and Dances - Volume 2
Hibiscus HLS-42. By John Ruffell
Club dance, fan dance, stick dance, and spear dance are included
volume 2. Recorded at the South Pacific Festival of the Arts.
Volume 1 is out of print.

Ha'aku'i Pele i Hawai'i! (Pele Prevails in Hawaii!) Aunty Edith Kanaka'ole
Hula HS-560.   1978
From the performer's family heritage, traditional plus more modern
composed chants are performed. Good notes with translations are
included.

Hawaiian Chant, Hula and Music Kaulaheaonamoku (Tom) Hiona
Folkways FW 8750.   1962
Vocal and instrumental music including the hula and traditional
chants; recording quality is not good, but the content is.

Island Music from the South Pacific
Nonesuch H-70288. By David Fanshawe 1981
Panpipes, nose flutes, drumming and a variety of songs and dances
from the island groups south of the Equator.

Morningtown Island Corroboree Songs various
W&G (Australia) WG-B 5007. By George Kansky
Music and songs that imitate dingoes, crocodiles, and other sounds
nature, plus selections of dijiridoo playing can be used to teach
lessons on animal sounds and sounds of nature cross-culturally.

Music from South New Guinea
Asch Mankind Series AHM 4216. By Wolfgang Laade 1971
Background information, notes, and notation of the melody are give
for each selection of vocal or instrumental music.

Polyphonies of the Solomon Islands
Le Chant du Monde LDX 74663. By Hugo Zemp 1978
Examples of vocal and instrumental polyphony of Guadalcanal and
Savo, in the Solomon Islands; recorded mainly at festivals.
Available from Earth Music.

The Gaugan Years
Nonesuch H-72017. By Francis Maziere
A broad survey of vocal and instrumental music including love song
a geneology recitation, hulas, and war songs, played on a variety of
instruments.

The Music of Hawaii
National Geographic 706. By Marc Aubort 1974
Documents pre-European styles of music as well as various types of
more current music, reaching below the veneer of tourist music
into the true traditions as performed by excellent musicians.

The Music of Tonga
National Geographic 3516. By Luis Marden 1972
Musical selections trace the history of Tonga, from canoe paddling chants to present day songs. Another outstanding recording by National Geographic.

Turou, Volume 2 Tereora College Ensemble
Electrotek (Rarotonga) EL 023 cass. 1978
Vocal and instrumental music of the Cook Islands performed by a lively ensemble and dance team.

PHILIPPINES

Bayanihan On Tour Bayanihan Ensemble
Monitor MFS 428.
A survey of styles, including gong music from the mountain areas. Song texts are given in Tagalog with English translations.

Bayanihan, Volume 1 Bayanihan Ensemble
Monitor MFS 322.
A folkloric presentation of traditional Philippine music and dance, with examples of Spanish influenced music including a rondalla.

Bayanihan, Volume 2 Bayanihan Ensemble
Monitor MFS 330. 1960
The survey includes two dances from the mountain provinces, Spanish influenced dances, and a Muslim dance plus a kulingtan piece.

Hanunoo Music From the Philippines
Folkways FE 4466. By Harold Conklin
Recorded examples of several different instruments; gongs, bamboo zithers, kolibit, kudyapi, jaws harp, and git git. Vocal music is also included in the recording.

Philippine Gong Music from Lanao 2 Volumes
Lyrichord LLST 7322, 26. By
Recordings of Kulingtan ensembles plus other instruments.

Tinikling Carmencita Y. Kazan
Kimbo LP 9015. By K.B.H. Productions 1972
Clear step by step instructions and music for the dance "Tinikling" are given on this record designed for educational use; suitable for grades 4 to 8.

SOUTH AMERICA

Batucada Fantastica Bossa Nova Os Ritmistas Brasileiros Orchestra
MGM SE 4085 also on RCA 1079001.
      Music of Carnival in the style of the escola de samba groups is a
reflection of Portuguese and African influences in Brazil.

Black Orpheus - Soundtrack A.C. Jobim and Luis Bonfa
Fontana SRF 67520.   1959
      This can be used as a listening lesson as the teacher uses the
music to illustrate the story of Black Orpheus, the Greek myth
of Orpheus transposed to the setting of Carnival in Rio de Janero.

Flutes des Andes Los Incas
Philips 6332 063.
      Indian music from the Andes; includes "El Condor Pasa" (s.1, b.2).
Simon and Garfunkel used the same song and musicians in **Bridge
Over Troubled Water** (s.1 b.2).

In Praise of Oxala and Other Gods - Black Music of South America
Nonesuch H-72036. By David Lewiston
      Colombia, Ecuador and Brazil were the sites of recordings
that illustrate African retentions in South American music.

Kingdom of the Sun
Nonesuch H-72029. By David Lewiston
      Music from Peru; s.1, b.4, a panpipes example, could be used as a
basis for student compositions on home made panpipes.

SOUTHEAST ASIA

Burmese Folk and Traditional Music Sien Be Dar
Folkways 4436. By Maung Than Myint
      A variety of instrumental and vocal music from both folk and art
music repertoires.

Cambodge: Musique Instrumentale
CBS (France) 65522. By Jacques Brunet 1973
      Four ensemble and five solo instrument pieces for various
occasions are recorded and documented with notes in French plus
photos.

Folk Songs of Viet Nam Pham Duy
Folkways FTS 31303. By Stephen Addiss 1968
      Westernized versions of folk and modern songs performed by Pham D
who was trained in France. Side 1 bands 5 through 7 are of more
traditional music.

Laos - Musique pour le khene, Lam Saravane   2 Volumes
Ocora 558.537,8. By Jaques Brunet 1982
>Volume 1 is music of the khen, volume 2 is of songs sung either in an alternating form or improvised, with khen accompaniment. Notes are included.

Les Mons De Thailande
CBS (France) 81389. By Hubert de Fraysseix 1976
>Examples of an ensemble which plays only for religious and magical ceremonies. A two page booklet provides background information.

Music of Cambodia - Musical Anthology of the Orient
Barenreiter BM 30 L 2002. By Alain Danelou
>Classical and folk music of various instruments, performed both as solos and in ensembles, plus some selections of vocal music are included, with notes on each selection.

Music of Viet Nam
Folkways FE 4352. By Pham Duy, S. Addiss, and W. Crofut 1965
>The short repeated xylophone pattern heard on s. 1. b. 1 could be notated for classroom use. Tribal, traditional and folk music are covered in this survey.

Musique Du Viet-nam, Tradition Du Sud Nguyen Vinh Bao and Tran Van Khe
Ocora OCR 68. By Tran Van Khe
>Easy to listen to, this makes a good introduction to the music of Viet Nam. Notes provide information on modes, tuning and instruments.

Musique Mnong Gar du Vietnam
Ocora OCR 80. By Georges Condominas 1958
>The examples of drumming, tube zither, and lithophone are particularly useful in the classroom.

Sounds of the World: Music of Southeast Asia
Music Educators National Conference. By Karl Signel 1982
>Three cassettes plus a study guide written by Patricia Shehan give suggestions for listening and teaching, with some translations and notation. Interviews may loose the students' interest.

Thailand - Lao Music of the Northeast
Lyrichord LLST 7357. By Terry E. Miller 1973
>Solo and ensemble music of the kaen (khen), plus male and female vocal music. Singers use fixed and improvised melodies. S.1, b. 4, 5 and 7 can be used for a comparison of styles among instruments.

The Traditional Music of Thailand 2 Volumes
IER IER 7502. By David Morton 1968
>Includes field recordings of all the important genres of Thai music. A 47 page booklet provides an introduction, commentary on the selections and analysis of the music.

[41]

Audio Visual

AFRICA - Sub-Saharan

Africa: Musical Instruments; Percussion, Strings, Wind
Warren Schloat   Format: film strips   1969
A series of three film strips on music with a teaching guide.
Basically a good series, giving examples from several different
parts of Africa, showing how the instruments are made and played.

Atumpan, the Talkng Drums of Ghana
UCLA   45 minutes   Format: 16 mm film or VHS   1964
An excellent film, narrated by Mantle Hood, shows the carving of a
royal set of drums for the Ashanti king, and their use in ceremonies
and dances. Available from UCLA or Original Music.

Discovering the Music of Africa
Arthur Barr Productions 19 minutes   Format: 16 mm, Video   1982
As a first introduction, the film is acceptable, however, it was
obviously filmed in a studio, plus it covers only the music of
Ghana, not Africa as a whole.

Fela In Concert
57 minutes   Format: VHS or Beta   1981
Filmed at a live concert in Paris, Fela and his troupe power
through some of his best known songs.
Available from Original Music.

ASIA - China, Japan, and Korea

A Night at the Peking Opera
Radim Films   20 minutes   Format: 16 mm color
Mime, costuming, singing, dance and acrobatics all combine to make
this an excellent introduction to Chinese music. Available from
the University of Washington Instructional Media Services.

Discovering the Music of Japan
Arthur Barr Productions   21 minutes   Format: 16 mm, Video   1982
Several instruments are introduced, plus historical background is provided. Performances of shakuhatchi, koto, and samisen, with vocal accompaniment, plus a dance performance.

Kodo: Heartbeat Drummers of Japan
Kinetic Film and Video   28 minutes   Format: 16 mm, VHS, Beta
A film that shows the training, both physical and mental, that are a part of the discipline of the musicians who form Kodo, a contemporary yet traditional taiko drum ensemble from Japan. Excellent.

Korean Folk Dances
University of Washington Press   25 minutes   Format: 16 mm   1969
Two folk dances, the tight rope dance, and the Farmer's dance, combine dance movements with strongly rhythmic music. Several other films on Korean Music and dance are available from UWP.

CARIBBEAN, CENTRAL AND SOUTH AMERICA

Discovering the Music of Latin America
Arthur Barr productions   Format: 16 mm, Video   1982
Covers Indian and Spanısh elements in the music of Latin America, but only once refers to any contribution from Africa. Filmed in a studio, it is a useful introduction if other information is added.

Music From Oil Drums
16 minutes   Format: 16 mm film   1957
An old film, but shows how steel drums are made, tuned and played. Available from the Audio Visual Center of Indiana University or the University of Washington Instructional Media Services.

INDIA

Discovering the Music of India
Arthur Barr Productions   21 minutes   Format: 16 mm, Video   1982
Music of both the South (Carnatic) and North (Hindustani) are introduced, with explanations of the melodic and rhythm structures. A traditional dance with song and gestures concludes this good film.

Famous Musicians: Ravi Shankar
Warren Schloat productions   Format: film strip
Not as exciting as seeing Shankar in action, but gives a picture of the man and his music. See also Shankar, **My Music, My Life.**

Folk Musicians of Rajasthan
UCLA   45 minutes   Format: VHS, Beta
  Folk traditions of northeast India, include songs, dances and
  rituals.

Folk Performers of India
UCLA   45 minutes   Format: VHS, Beta
  Nine different views of Indian folk traditions include magic acts,
  puppetry, acrobatics, impersonation, and other acts accompanied by
  music, with explanatory narrative.

God With A Green Face
American Society for Eastern Arts   Format: 16 MM
  The intensive training and riveting performances of the Kathakali
  dance drama of southern India provide a new experience for students
  Available from the Center for World Music, San Diego State Univers

INDONESIA

Indonesian Dance Drama
UCLA 30+ minutes   Format: VHS or U-Matic
  Incorporating short presentations of the Balinese shadow play,
  the three dimensional puppets of Java, a dance drama and
  Sundanese masked dances. Available from UCLA or Original Music.

Serama's Mask
Coronet Films and Video 25 minutes   Format: 16 mm, Video   1979
  A Balinese teenager practices the traditional masked dances of
  Bali and carves the mask he is to wear in the performance that will
  be his father's last. An excellent film.

ISRAEL AND THE JEWISH DIASPORA

A Life of Song
Cindy Marshall Productions 38 minutes   Format: Video
  Yiddish folk songs by Ruth Rubin.

NORTH AFRICA AND THE MIDDLE EAST

Discovering the Music of the Middle East
Arthur Barr Productions 20 minutes   Format: 16mm, Video   1970
  Narrated by a woman, the film covers several instruments and
  styles of music and discusses how the spread of Islam has been an
  influence. Ornamentation and asymmetrical rhythms are demonstrate

[44]

Musical Instruments of the Near East
Near East Resource Center, University of Washington Format: slides and tape
Slides and tape provide the sounds of several instruments of the
Near East.

NORTH AMERICA

Chulas Fronteras
59 minutes   Format: 16 mm, VHS, Beta 1966
Chicano musicians play conjunto music of the Nortena style, with
background on lifestyle and the hardship of the farm worker's life.
Available from Original Music or U. of W. Instructional Media.

Discovering American Folk Music
Arthur Barr Productions   Format: 16 mm, Video 1982
The music of Britain and Africa are traced as the most important
components making up the music of America. Songs are traced to
show changes, and other influences are demonstrated musically.

Discovering American Indian Music
Arthur Barr Productions 24 minutes   Format: 16 mm, Video 1971
A good survey of many types of Indian music and dance, mostly from
the plains and Southwest areas, but also including one Tlinkit dance
and contemporary Indian music by Louis Ballard.

Discovering Country Western Music
Arthur Barr Productions   Format: 16 mm, Video 1982
Traces how the folk music of the mountain people of the south has
evolved into an urbanized, popular music, for the mass media
including radio, records and movies.

Discovering Jazz
Arthur Barr Productions 22 minutes   Format: 16 mm, Video 1969
An historical approach to jazz, (which tends to loose student
interest), filmed in a studio.

In the Land of The War Canoes
University of Washington Press 47 minutes   Format: 16 mm B&W 1973
An outstanding film made in 1914 by Edward S. Curtis of a fictional
love story between a Kwakiutl man and woman, with a new but authentic soundtrack added; based on Kwakiutl life and legends.

Roots of American Music: Country and Urban Blues 3 Parts
University of Washington Press   Format: 16 mm film
Part I and part II are a series of performances by famous blues
musicians, each a separate performance, 40 minutes, and 35 minutes,
Part III - Fred McDowell 23 minutes.

OCEANIA

Hawaiian Musical Instruments
Bishop Museum   Format: slides and tape
A set of slides showing various instruments of Hawaii; big hits
are the dog tooth rattle and the nose flute. Other films and
AV materials are available from the Bishop Museum.

PHILIPPINES

Music and Dance of the Manobo and Bagobo of Mindanau
University of Washington Press   12 minutes   Format: 16 mm   1970
Pre-Hispanic, Pre-Moslem traditions still survive on Mindanao,
where gong music is performed using sets of tuned, bossed gongs.

Music and Dances of the Yakan Peoples of the Basilan Islands
University of Washington Press   12 minutes   Format: 16mm   1970
A Moslem people, the Yakan live on the southern island of Zamboang
in the Philippines. Three war dances, a kulingtang ensemble, and
other instrumental performances are featured.

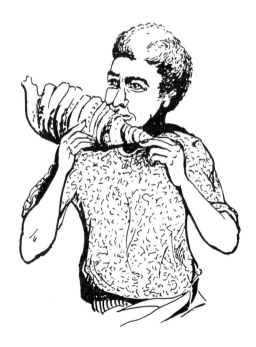

Archives

Archive of Folksong,
   Library of Congress Washington, DC 20540

Archive of Folk Culture, American Folklife Center
   Library of Congress Washington DC 20540
      "Folklife Sourcebook", a directory of folklife organizations; "LC Folk
      Archive Reference Aid - Recording Companies" plus other publications.

Archive of Southwestern Music, Fine Arts Library
   University of New Mexico Albaquerque, NM 87106
      Spanish American and Native American materials.

Archives of Ethnic Music and Dance, School of Music - Ethnomusicology
   University of Washington, Seattle WA 98195
      Films on music and dance from Korea, the Philippines, and the USA.

Archives of Traditional Music, School of Music
   Indiana University Bloomington IN 47401
      An extensive collection of ethnomusicologists' field recordings.

British Library National Sound Archive, Ms. Lucy Duran
   29 Exhibition Road London SW7 2AS G. B.
      Offer recordings, reference library, information service, plus
      assistance with field work, and tape duplication service.

Canadian Centre for Folk Culture Studies,
   National Museum of Man Ottawa, Ontario Canada
      Folk song archive, instrument collection, plus publications.

John Edwards Memorial Foundation, Folklore and Mythology Center
   11369 Bunche Hall   UCLA Los Angeles, CA 90024
      Archives of recordings of blues, country and folk music, plus
      some transcriptions are available.

Library of Congress, Music Division, Recorded Sound Section
   Washington, D.C. 20540
      Write for a catalog of available recordings.

Program in Ethnomusicology, Department of Music
   University of California Los Angeles, CA 90024
      Books, monographs, scholarly reports, records, films and video
      cassettes of their own production.

University of Michigan, School of Music
    Ann Arbor, MI 48109

University of Texas Folklore Archives, Social Work Building, #306,
    University of Texas, Austin, TX 78712

Organizations

Asian Cultural Centre for UNESCO,
6, Fukuromachi, Shinjuku-ku, Tokyo 162 Japan
Books, recordings and a periodical bulletin on Asian music
and culture - see the discography for specific titles.

Australian Institute of Aboriginal Studies,
Box 553 City P.O., Canberra, A.C.T., 2600 Australia
catalog of publications

Bishop Museum, Education Dept.,
P.O. Box 6037, Honolulu, HI 96818
Publications, films, slides and other materials on music
of the Pacific.

Canadian Folk Music Society,,
15 Julien St., Pointe Claire, Quebec, Canada

Center for Intercultural Studies in Folklore and Oral History, American Folklife Society
University of Texas, Austin TX 78712

Chinese Information Service,
159 Lexington Ave., New York, NY 10016
brochures and pamphlets on Chinese music, art and history.

Chinese Music Society of North America,
2339 Charmingfare, Woodridge, IL 60517-2910
journal

College Music Society,
Regent Box 44, University of Colorado, Boulder, CO 80309

Committee for the Preservation and Study of Hawaiian Language, Art and Culture
University of Hawaii, 2411 Dole St., Honolulu, HI 96822

Country Music Association Inc.,
7 Music Circle N., Nashville TN 37203
Offers information on country music, promotes the country music
industry.

Country Music Foundation,
700 16th Ave. S., Nashville, TN 37203
"Journal of Country Music"

El Centro Campesino Cultural,
   Box 1278 San Juan Batista, CA 95045

International Council For Traditional Music, Department of Music
   Columbia University, New York, NY 10027
   "Yearbook for Traditional Music"

International Folk Music Council,
   Music Dept., Queens University, Kingston, ONT. Canada K7M 6R2
      Associated with UNESCO, to encourage the study and preservation
      of folk music and dance.

International Society for Music Education, Music School
   University of Canterbury, Christchurch 1, New Zealand 03554231

American Folklore Society,
   1703 New Hampshire Ave., NW, Washington DC 20009
   "Journal of American Folklore"

Music Educators National Conference, Multi-cultural Awareness Committee
   1902 Association Drive, Reston, VA 22091

National Council for the Traditional Arts,
   1346 Connecticut Ave. NW #1118, Washington, DC 20036

National Geographic Society,
   P.O. Box 2118, Washington DC 20013-2118
      maps of ethnic groups, record series.

Office of International Arts Affairs,
   Department of State, Washington, DC 20560

Smithsonian Institution, Office of Folklife Programs
   955 L'Enfant Plaza SW, Suite 2600, Washington, DC 20560

Society for Ethnomusicology,
   Ethnomusicology Program, Indiana University, 506 North Fess Ave., Bloomington IN 4740
      Ethnomusicology Journal and Newsletter
      Education committee

The Asia Society,
   725 Park Avenue, New York, NY 10021
      "Focus" magazine, with special issues on music, crafts and other
      folk arts.

The Society for Asian Music, Hagop Kevorkian Center
   50 Washington Square South, New York, NY 10012
      journal - "Asian Music"

UNESCO: United Nations Educational, Scientific and Cultural Organization,
   7 place de Fontenoy, 75700 Paris, France

UNICEF - The United States Committee,
   331 East 38th St., New York, NY 10016
      Their catalog includes some books and records on world music,
      including the **Sing, Children Sing** series.
The World Music Institute
   155 West 72 St., Suite 706, New York, NY 10023
      Non-profit; sponsors ethnic festivals and concert series, mail order service for book
      and recordings.

Book Sellers

Children's Book and Music Center,
2500 Santa Monica Blvd. Santa Monica, CA 90404
A catalog lists their books and records for sale, including
folk music, world music, and dance.

Ethnographic Arts Publications,
1040 Erica Rd. Mill Valley, CA 94941
Rare and out of print books.

Heinrichshofen -Books, Florian Noetzel Verlag
P.O. Box 580 D-2940 Wilhelmshaven, Federal Republic of Germany
journal - "The World of Music"

International Book and Record Distributors,
40-11 24th St., LIC New York 11101
SN   PL

Kinokuniya Bookstores,
1581 Webster St., San Francisco, CA 94115
Books and records on Japan and Japanese music and culture.

Legacy Books,
P.O. Box 494 Hatboto, PA 19040
A specialist bookseller, offering titles on folklore, ethnomusicology,
dance, folk music and other related fields of interest.

Original Music,
RD 1, Box 190 Lasher Rd., Tivoli, NY 12583
Write for their catalog listing world music recordings, books
and videos. Outstanding choices and many hard to find titles.

Sing Out!,
Box 1071, Easton, PA 18042
A bimonthly periodical that covers all aspects of North American
music. Reprints of songs available also.

Tara Publications,
29 Derby Ave. Cedarhurst, NY 11516
"A Harvest of Jewish Music" - catalog of books, records
and tapes concerning Jewish music.

The Book Bin - Hawaii,
   351 NW Jackson St., Corvallis, OR 97330
      Books on Hawaii and the Pacific.

The Cellar Book Shop,
   18090 Wyoming, Detroit, Michigan 48221
      Books on the Philippines, Asia, the Pacific, Australia and
      New Zealand.

The Shorey Book Store,
   110 Union St., Seattle WA 98104
      Out of print and rare books, Northwest Indian music and
      culture, rare book searches.

Theodore Front Musical Literature,
   16122 Cohasset St., Van Nuys CA 91406
      Write for their catalog of titles relating to ethnomusicology.

World Around Songs,
   Route 5   Burnsville, NC 28714
      A series of little song books, covering just about every area of the
      world, plus some collections from several areas.

World Music Press,
   P.O. Box 2565 Danbury, CT 06813
      Music, books, and recordings relating to world music geared toward
      teachers' needs.

RECORD LABELS - ABBREVIATIONS

AF - Afrotone
AM - A & M
AN - Anthology
AR - Arhoolie
AS - Asylum
BB - BBC
BG - Blue Goose
BL - Blue Note
BM - Barenreiter-Musicaphon
CA - Carino
CF - Chulas Fronteras
CH - Chess Records
CM - Chante du Monde
CO - Columbia
CS - City Sounds
DI - Discolor
DY - Dyno

EP - Epic
EU - Eurotone
FO - Folklyric
GA - Gallo
HI - Hibiscus
MC - MCA
ME - Menyah
NO - Nonesuch
OC - Ocora
PL - Playa Sound
SA - Salsoul
SO - Sonet
SN - Sonodisc
SP - Sparrow
TE - Testament
VA - Vaya
VO - Vogue

[53]

Record Companies

A B C Records,
    70 Universal City Plaza
    Universal City, CA 91608
    Other labels: MCA

Arhoolie Records,
    10341 San Pablo Ave.,
    El Cerrito, CA 94530
    Other labels: AR CF FO PL
        also Down Home Music

Atlantic Records,
    75 Rockefeller Plaza
    New York, NY 10019

B & F Record Company,
    3046 East 123rd St.,
    Cleveland, OH 44120

Banjar Records, Box 32164
    7440 University Ave., N.E.
    Minneapolis, MN 55432

BBC Records, distr. by: RTV Sales Corp.

Biograph Records,
    16 River St.,
    Chatham, NY 12037

Blue Note, distr. by: Manhattan Records

Caedmon Records,
    1995 Broadway
    New York, NY 10023

Canyon Records,
    4143 N. 16th Ave.,
    Phoenix, AZ 85016

Capitol Records Inc.,
    1750 N. Vine St.,
    Hollywood, CA 90028
    Other labels: SP

CBS Records,
    51 West 52nd St.,
    New York, NY 10019
    Other labels: CO EP

Chante du Monde, distr. by: Harmon▪

Coco Records Inc.,
    1650-1700 Broadway
    New York, NY 10019

Elektra,
    75 Rockefeller Plaza
    New York, NY 10019
    Other labels: AS NO

Everest Records,
    2020 Avenue of the Stars
    Century City, CA 90067

Fania Records, Inc.,
    888 Seventh Ave.,
    New York, NY 10019
    Other labels: VA

antasy Records,
    Tenth and Parker
    Berkeley, CA 94710

estival Records,
    2769 West Pico Blvd.,
    Los Angeles, CA 90006

fth Continent Music Co.,,
    1200 Newell Hill Pl., #302
    Walnut Creek, CA 94596

olklyric, distr. by: Arhoolie

olkways Records, (now Folkways/Smithsonian)
    Birchtree Group,
    Box 2072, Princeton, NJ 08540

allo, distr. by: Qualiton Imports

armonia Mundi USA Inc.,,
    3364 South Robertson Blvd.,
    Los Angeles, CA 90034
    Other labels: CM   OC

dian House,
    Box 472
    Taos, NM 87571

ternational Record Industries, Inc.,
    P.O. Box 593 Radio City Station
    New York, NY 10019
    Other labels: BM   AF

oqrafts Ltd.,
    RR #2
    Ohsweken, Ont. Canada

sland Records Inc.,,
    444 Madison Ave.,
    New York, NY 10022

Jazz Archives,
    333 West 52nd St.,
    New York, NY 10019

Kaleidoscope Records,
    Box 0
    El Cerrito, CA 94530

Kicking Mule,
    Box 158
    Alderpoint, Ca 95411
    Other labels: SO

Kimbo,
    Box 477
    Long Branch, NJ 07740

Kiwi Pacific Records Ltd.,,
    Murray Vincent, Production Manager
    P.O. Box 826 Wellington, New Zealand
    Other labels: HI

Kubaney Publishing, Discolor Records
    4728 N.W. 167th St.,
    Miami Lakes, FL 33014
    Other labels: DI

Latin Percussion,
    160 Belmont Ave.,
    Garfield, NJ 07026
    Other labels: instructional recordings

Lyrichord,
    141 Perry St.,
    New York, NY 10014

Mango Records,
    7720 Sunset Blvd.,
    Los Angeles, CA 90046

Manhattan Records,
    1370 Avenue of the Americas
    New York, NY 10019
    Other labels: BL

MMO Music Group Inc.,
    50 S. Buckhout St.,
    Irvington, NY 10533
    Other labels: CS CH VO

Monitor Records,
    156 Fifth Ave.,
    New York, NY 10010

Music of Polynesia,
    1441 Kapiolani Blvd,
    Honolulu, HI 96814

New World Records,
    701 Seventh Ave.
    New York, NY 10036

Nonesuch Records, distr. by: Elektra
    75 Rockefeller Plaza
    New York, NY 10019

Origin Jazz Library,
    Box 85
    Santa Monica, CA 90406
    Other labels: TE

Philips, distr. by: Polygram Classics

Polydor, distr. by: Polygram

Polygram Records - Polygram Classics,
    810 Seventh Ave.
    New York, NY 10019

RCA Records,
    1133 Avenue of the Americas
    New York, NY 10036
    Other labels: AM SA

Records International,
    Box 1140
    Goleta, CA 93116

Rounder Records,
    One Camp St.,
    Cambridge, MA 02140

RTV Sales Corp.,
    4375 SW 60th Ave.,
    Fort Lauderdale, FL 33314
    Other labels: BBC

Salsoul Records, distr. by RCA

Shanachie Records,
    Dalebrook Park
    Ho-Ho-Kus, NJ 07423

Sheffield Lab Inc.,
    Box 5332
    Santa Barbara, CA 93108
    Other labels: compact discs

Testament Records, distr. by: Origin

University of Washington Press,
    Box 85569
    Seattle WA 98195

Vogue Records, distr. by: Rounder

Yazoo Records,
    245 Waverly Pl.,
    New York, NY 10014
    Other labels: BG

Record Vendors

Anthology Record and Tape Company,
    135 West 41st St., New York, NY 10036
    African and Asian music

Audio Research Services, Inc.,
    739 Boylston St., Boston, Mass. 02116
    AF   AN   BM   EU   OC

Balkan Record Distributing Company,
    R.D. #2, Concord Church Rd., Beaver Falls, PA 15010

Children's Music Center,
    2500 Santa Monica Blvd., Santa Monica, CA 90404
    A catalog lists their books and records for sale including folk
    music, world music, and dance.

Express Music Catalog,
    175 Fifth Ave., New York, NY 10010
    Order records by mail or by phone - 1 800 233-6357.

Floyd's Record Shop,
    Post Drawer 10, Ville Platte LA 70586
    Recordings of Cajun and Creole music, including Swallow records.

Folk-Legacy Records Inc.,
    Sharon Mountain Road,, Sharon, CT 06069

House of Musical Traditions,
    7040 Carrol Ave., Takoma Park, MD 20912
    Books, recordings and ethnic musical instruments. Write for
    their catalog.

Interculture Associates,
    Box 277, Thompson, CT 06277
    Records, instruments, books, and films, with an emphasis on India.

International Book and Record Distributors,
    40-11 24th St., LIC New York 11101
    SN   PL

Original Music,
RD 1, Box 190 Lasher Rd., Tivoli, NY 12583
Write for their catalog listing world music recordings, books and videos. They offer custom cassettes of rare recordings.

Qualiton Imports,
39-28 Crescent St., Long Island, NY 11101
GA

Roundup Records,
P.O. Box 154, N. Cambridge, MA 02140
Many of the smaller and international labels are available from their catalog.

Tower Records,
692 Broadway,, New York, NY 10012
Any record in print, plus videos are available by mail or by telephone: 1-800-522-5445.

World Music Press,
P.O. Box 2565, Danbury, CT 06813
Several recordings relating to world music and useful to teachers are available from their catalog.

Media Companies

Audio Visual Center,
 Indiana University Bloomington, IN 47401

Arthur Barr Productions, P.O. Box 5667,
 3490 East Foothill Blvd., Pasadena, CA 91107
 The "Discovering the Music of..." series, originally from Bailey
 Film Associates is now available on film or video.

Bilingual Media Productions,
 P.O. Box 9337 North Berkeley Stn. Berkeley, CA 94709

Center For Southern Folklore,
 3756 Mimosa Ave., Memphis, TN 38111
 Films, records, photographs, and books concerning the folk
 culture of the South.

Churchill Films,
 622 N. Robertson Blvd., Los Angeles, CA 90069

Cindy Marshall Productions,
 76 Columbus Ave. Somerville, Mass. 02143

Coronet Films & Video,
 108 Wilmot Road, Deerfield, IL 60015

EAV Educational Audio Visual Inc.,
 Pleasantville, NY 10570

Educational Film Library Association,
 43 W. 61st St., New York, NY 10023
 Information service for finding films, or suggest films to fit
 individual needs.

Films Incorporated,
 5447 N. Ravenswood Ave., Chicago, II 60640-1199
 film or video - **Banjo Man**

G.P.N. Media, George Lillyman
 764 Pleasant Ave., Tulare, CA 93274
 Musical Instruments series of videos includes Africa and South
 America; **The Music Machine** series includes Japan and Africa.

Kinetic Film - Video,
255 Delaware Ave., Suite 340 Buffalo, NY 14202

Learning Corporation of America,
711 Fifth Ave. New York, NY 10022
film - **Black Music in America - From Then Till Now.**

Original Music,
RD 1, Box 190 Lasher Rd. Tivoli, NY 12583
Write for their catalog listing world music recordings,
books and videos. Outstanding choices.

Program in Ethnomusicology, Department of Music
University of California Los Angeles, CA 90024
Books, monographs, scholarly reports, records, films and
video cassettes of their own production.

Radim Films,
430 W. Grand Pl., Chicago, IL 60614

The Asia Society,
725 Park Avenue, New York, NY 10021
Videos, films, slides, publications and records are available from
the society.

University of Oklahoma Productions, Indian Education
106 E. Const. Norman, OK 73069

University of Washington, Instructional Media Center
35 D Kane Hall, DG-10, Seattle, WA 98195
Films and videos may be rented.

University of Washington, Near East Resource Center
219 Denny Hall (DH-20) Seattle, WA 98195
The center offers bibliographies, films, video tapes, slides and a speaker
bureau on the cultures of the Near East.

University of Washington Press,
Box 85569 Seattle WA 98195
Write for a catalog of their books, records and films, which includes
a series of films from the Archives of Ethnic Music and Dance.

World Music Press
P.O. Box 2565, Danbury CT 06813
Publishers and distributors of authentic, in-depth yet accessible multicultural books,
recordings videos and choral music. Send for catalog.

Instruments

Carroll Sound Inc.,
   351 West 41st St., New York, NY 10036
      Steel drums, percussion, and other ethnic instruments.

Matt Finstrom,
   5975 W. Western Way, Box 116-B, Tucson, AZ   85713
      Custom built instruments, including balafons, tuned gongs, kalimbas,
      birimbaos, and shakuhachis.

House of Musical Traditions,
   7040 Carrol Ave., Takoma Park, MD 20912
      Ethnic musical instruments, plus books, and recordings.   Write
      for their catalog.

Hula Supply Center,
   2346 King St., Honolulu, HI 96822
      Musical instruments and hula supplies.

Interculture Associates,
   Box 277, Thompson, CT 06277
      Instruments, records, books, films, with an emphasis on India.

Jag Drums,
   88 Hibbert St., Arlington, MA 02174
      Authentic Ewe barrel drums, donno and brekete drums, plus
      axatse, gankogui, and mbiras.

John's Music Center,
   5521-A University Way N.E., Seattle, WA 98105
      Ethnic instruments from around the world, plus ethnic music
      publications, music education materials, and Orff instruments.

Knock on Wood Xylophones,
   RD 2 Box 790, Thorndike MA 04986
      Beautiful hand made xylophones of American hardwoods, with rope
      framework; perfect for the classroom.

Lark In The Morning,
   P.O. Box 1176 Mendocino, CA 95460
      Instruments, newsletter, catalog, books, videos; mainly
      related to American and European folk traditions.

Latin Percussion,
160 Belmont Ave., Garfield, NJ 07026
Latin percussion instruments, plus instructional recordings.

Peripole Inc.,
Browns Mills, NJ 08015-0146
Music education instruments and materials, including some ethnic instruments and Orff instruments.

Rhythm Band Inc.,
P.O. Box 126 Fort Worth, TX 76101-0126
Ethnic musical instruments, some with instruction booklets plus autoharps and other music education materials and instruments.

ADDENDA:
Books
Bierhorst, John
1979 **A Cry from the Earth**
New York: Four Winds Press. 113 pages
Music of the North American Indians. Transcriptions, in-depth but non-technical annotation dealing with all culture areas and many genres of Native American music.
Photos. (out-of-print but avail. in most libraries) Folkways LP FA 37777 (just reissued).
Kenney, Maureen
1983 **Circle Round the Zero**
St. Louis: Magnamusic-Baton, Inc. 73 pages.
Play chants and singing games of city children. Ball bouncing, clap, jump rope, etc.
Roberts, John Storm
1972 **Black Music of Two Worlds**
New York: Original Music (pbk reprint 198-) 282 pages
Comprehensive guide to the black music of Africa, North and South America and the Caribbean. Companion LP listed separately.
198? **The Latin Tinge**
New York: Original Music. 238 pages.
History of the profound influence of Latin music in the United States, including a look at salsa and Chicano music. Rare photos.
Tanna, Laura
1984 **Jamaican Folk Tales and Oral Histories**
Kingston, Jamaica: Institute of Jamaica Publications, Ltd. 143 pages.
Performance and cultural background information, photos, stories never before published, many stories inc. songs. Pbk.; Hdcv; Tape; Video. Avail. World Music Press.

Recordings
Canciones de me Tierra
Arhoolie 3024. By Los Campesinos de Michoacan.
Variety of Mexican song styles played on violins, harp, vihuela, jarana, voices.
Chinese Folk Songs
Lyrichord LLST 7152. By Lui Hung and traditional Chinese Orchestra.
Instruments include cheng, erhu, pipa, percussion, others. Solo singer. Brief notes.
Flute Songs of the Kiowa and Comanche
Indian House IH 2512-C. By Tom Mauchahty-Ware.
Traditional tunes played in the open air on a cedar flute. Cass. includes notes.
Georgia Sea Island Songs
New World Records 278. By the original Georgia Sea Island Singers (Bessie Jones et al.)
Spirituals, shouts, ballads, work songs, laments. Good notes by Lomax.
Israel Dances
Folkways FW 6935. By the Tzabar Group.
Israeli folk dances performed by a well-known Israeli group. Sung in Hebrew. Notes include Hebrew, English transliteration and English translation, dance steps.
Love Songs of the Lakota
Indian House IH 4315. By Kevin Locke
Traditional Lakota Sioux love tunes played on wooden flutes. Cass. includes notes.
Music from the People's Republic of China
Rounder Records 4008. (1976) By Honan Theatrical School; Hupeh Opera Troupe.
Young people perform traditional and modern (more political) works.
Return on Wings of Pleasure
Rounder Records 5003. By Pedro Padilla y su Conjunto.
Traditional Puerto Rican instrumental and vocal selections. Excellent notes.
Sounds of the World: Music of Latin America (Mexico, Ecuador, Brazil)
Music Educators National Conference. 3 Tapes produced by Karl Signell.
Booklet by Dale Olsen, Daniel Sheehy, Charles Perrone. includes background information, suggestions for use.
The Indestructible Beat of Soweto
Shanachie 43033. By various contemporary South African groups.
Excellent overview of current (1981-84) South African township pop styles.

Is multicultural music exciting to you?

Copy this coupon to order additional copies of *World Music: A Source Book for Teaching*—**or any of these other unique and refreshing World Music Press publications:**

Yes! Please send me:

Quantity:

_____*A Singing Wind: Five Melodies from Ecuador* **$6.95**

companion tape $4.95_____

_____*Let Your Voice Be Heard! Songs from Ghana and Zimbabwe,* by Abraham Kobena Adzinyah, Dumisani Maraire and Judith Cook Tucker, $14.95; companion tape $8.50_____Set $20.95_____

_____*Songs and Stories from Uganda,* by W. Moses Serwadda, illustrated by Leo and Diane Dillon, Narrated by Moriah Vecchia, $12.95 Book (two-colors throughout); companion tape $5.95_____; Set $17.95_____

_____*Teaching Asian Musics in the Elementary and Secondary School,* by William Anderson (An intro. to the music of India and Indonesia), $7.95 ; companion tape $6

_____*Teaching the Music of Six Different Cultures,* by Luvenia A. George, $14.95 Companion tape $7.95_____ (set $21.50)_____

_____*Step It Down,* by Bessie Jones and Bess Lomax Hawes, $10.95 (pbk)

_____*World Music: A Source Book for Teaching* $7.95

$_____SUB-TOTAL + s/h = $_____TOTAL (Check or PO)

(Please add $1.50 s/h for first book or set; 50¢ for each additional book or set; CT residents add 7 1/2% sales tax.)

Name_____

Address _____

City _____ **State   Zip** _____

_____*Please send me your current catalog! (Get one for a friend, too!)*

Send to: World Music Press, PO Box 2565,
Danbury CT 06813 **(203) 748-1131**

Multicultural Materials for Educators - *our only focus*
[Or order from your favorite bookstore or music dealer!]

(Libraries:Please order Let Your Voice Be Heard! from
Quality Books, Inc)